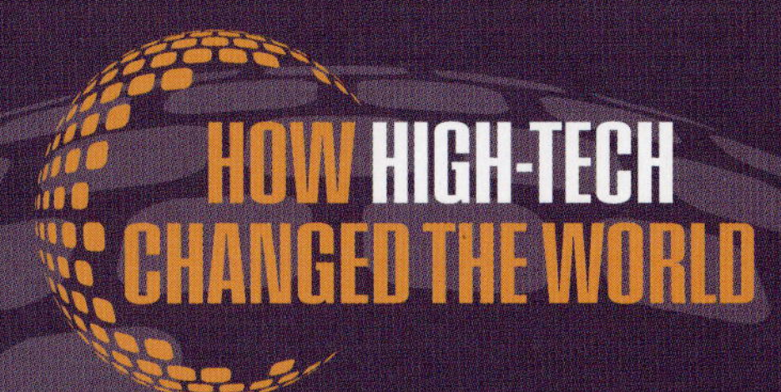

GPS

Published in 2025 by **Cheriton Children's Books**
1 Bank Drive West, Shrewsbury, Shropshire, SY3 9DJ

© Copyright 2025 Cheriton Children's Books

First Edition

Author: Kelly Roberts
Designer: Paul Myerscough
Editor: Jennifer Sanderson
Proofreader: Amy Strauss
Consultant: David Hawksett, BSc

Picture credits: Cover: Shutterstock/Evgeny Vasenev (t), Shutterstock/DenPhotos (c), Shutterstock/PressLab (bl), Shutterstock/Cavan Images (br). Inside: p4: Shutterstock/Africa Studio, p5: Shutterstock/Simona Pilolla 2, p6: Shutterstock/Everett Collection, p7: Shutterstock/Andrei Armiagov, p8: Shutterstock/Miljan Zivkovic, p9: Shutterstock/Phonlamai Photo, p10: Wikimedia Commons/USAF, p11: Shutterstock/Rocksweeper, p12b: Wikimedia Commons/Gregory R Todd, p12t: Shutterstock/PressLab, p13: Shutterstock/Mark Reinstein, p14: Shutterstock/Gorodenkoff, p15b: Shutterstock/Getmilitaryphotos, p15t: Shutterstock/PeopleImages.com/Yuri A, p16: Shutterstock/PressLab, p17: Shutterstock/Gorodenkoff, p18: Shutterstock/Ivan Cholakov, p19: Shutterstock/Gorodenkoff, p20: Shutterstock/One Photo, p21: Wikimedia Commons/USAF, p22: Shutterstock/Patryk Kosmider, p23: Shutterstock/Gorodenkoff, p24: Shutterstock/Sculpies, p25: Shutterstock/Bjoern Wylezich, p26: Shutterstock/Maridav, p27: Shutterstock/Cast Of Thousands, p28: Shutterstock/Ground Picture, p29: Wikimedia Commons/USAF/Adrian Cadiz, p30: Shutterstock/Scott Prokop, p31: Shutterstock/Metamorworks, p32: MIT Museum, p33b: Shutterstock/Toa55, p33t: Shutterstock/Cavan-Images, p34: Shutterstock/Everst, p35: Shutterstock/Georgid, p36b: Shutterstock/Fly and Dive, p36t: Shutterstock/Somkanae Sawatdinak, p37: Wikimedia Commons/NASA, p38: Shutterstock/Mr. Amarin Jitnathum, p39: Shutterstock/Kaspars Grinvalds, p40: Shutterstock/Andrey Popov, p41: Shutterstock/Lassedesignen, p42: Shutterstock/TUKiphoto, p43: Wikimedia Commons/Ferdinand Schmutzer, p44: Shutterstock/Andrei Armiagov, p45: Shutterstock/Gorodenkoff.

All rights reserved. No part of this book may be reproduced in any form without permission of the publisher, except by a reviewer.

Printed in China

Please visit our website,
www.cheritonchildrensbooks.com
to see more of our high-quality books.

CONTENTS

CHAPTER 1

THE GPS STORY

The Global Positioning System (GPS) is a network of high-tech satellites that allows people to find their position anywhere on our planet. Anyone with a GPS receiver can pick up the signals from these satellites to pinpoint their location on Earth.

Made up of Three Parts

The GPS consists of three parts or segments. The "space segment" is the network of satellites that zooms around in space, thousands of miles above Earth's surface. These satellites beam radio signals down to our planet and connect with the "user segment"—anyone with a GPS receiver. Finally, the "control segment" is the part that maintains the satellites in orbit around Earth.

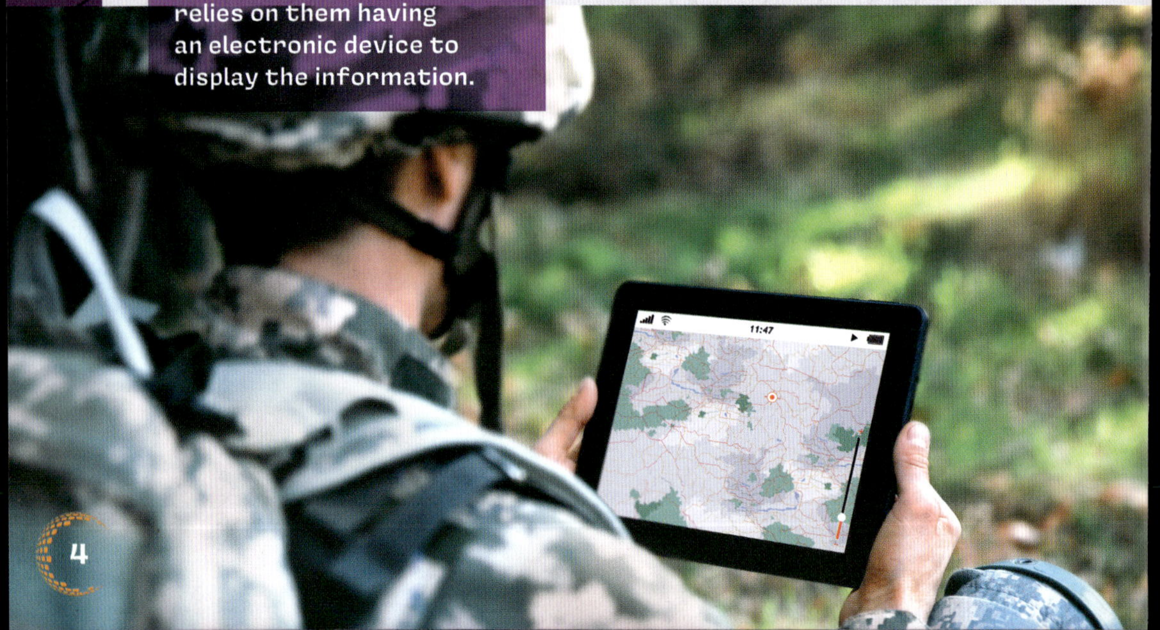

Finding a location with GPS is very useful for a soldier, but the technology relies on them having an electronic device to display the information.

Made in America

The GPS is an American invention developed for military forces. GPS helps soldiers find their way in unfamiliar territory and allows military commanders to plan their operations. It also guides missiles to their targets. In 1983, the US government made GPS available for everyone to use. At first, public GPS signals were made weaker than military signals and the public GPS was not very accurate. This changed in 2000, when the government stopped making public signals weaker. Overnight, GPS became far more accurate for all users.

Planning a route with GPS is far quicker than using a paper map.

A Technology That Changed the World

Today, anyone can pinpoint their location on Earth and find their way around using a GPS-enabled device. GPS receivers are built into many electronic gadgets, ranging from smartphones to car navigation systems. In this book we'll discover more about the technology that makes the GPS work. We'll also explore the history of GPS, how it has changed your world, and the brilliant scientists behind this incredible invention.

HOW HIGH-TECH CHANGED THE WORLD

Before GPS became available for everyone, people used paper maps and road signs to find their way around. And before then, people navigated using a compass, natural landmarks, or the position of the sun and stars in the sky. Planning a long journey by road once involved a lot of time looking in detail at maps, taking notes, and planning stops for fuel and refreshments. With GPS, this now takes just a few seconds.

How GPS Works

The GPS is a series of satellites that spin around Earth in space. There are currently more than 30 satellites in operation. They send radio signals to GPS receivers on Earth, and can be used to track the movement of objects anywhere on the surface of our planet.

Using Satellites

Each GPS satellite is about 18 feet (5.5 m) long and weighs about 1.5 tons (1.3 mt). The satellites travel about 16,500 miles (26,600 km) above Earth's surface at speeds of up to 9,000 miles per hour (14,000 kph). It takes each satellite about 12 hours to make just one complete journey—which is called an orbit—around Earth. A satellite will only be able to communicate with a person if the satellite is above their horizon. To overcome this problem, satellite networks or "constellations" are used.

HIGH-TECH HISTORY

The first in the fleet of GPS satellites, Navstar 1, was launched in 1978, followed by ten more just like it. Their solar panels could generate 400 watts of power. Since the 1978 launch, there have been many improvements in the design of GPS satellites. The most recently launched are seventh-generation satellites, called Block III satellites. More than half a dozen Block III satellites have been launched. They can generate ten times the power of Navstar 1. The Block III satellites are named for significant people in the history of navigation, including Ferdinand Magellan (1480–1521), Neil Armstrong (1930–2012), and Amelia Earhart (1897–1937).

Amelia Earhart became the first woman to fly solo across the Atlantic Ocean.

At any one time, there are 24 active satellites orbiting Earth. The remaining are spares in case one of the other satellites fails. Altogether, more than 80 satellites have been launched.

Powered by the Sun

GPS satellites have huge solar panels to trap the energy from the sun. These panels extend out from the satellite like two wings, each measuring about 18 feet (5.5 m) long. Light-sensitive cells on the solar panels convert light energy into electricity. This is then used to power the satellite systems and send radio signals back down to Earth. The satellites also have nickel-hydrogen batteries as a backup power supply.

Costly Technology

Sending satellites into space is extremely expensive. It currently costs around $330 million for each of the latest generation of GPS satellites, including the cost of research and improvements. The Delta rockets that carry the satellites into space cost at least $164 million to build and launch. Keeping the satellites in space is no less expensive—it costs approximately $2 million per day to run the GPS satellite system.

Beamed to Earth

GPS satellites beam radio signals to receivers on Earth's surface. These signals give information about the satellites' positions. Each satellite carries a highly accurate atomic clock, which shows what time the signals were sent. GPS satellites transmit radio signals at regular intervals, and the atomic clock on the satellite ensures the signals are synchronized. This means that each satellite sends the signals at exactly the same time.

GPS satellites can communicate directly with smartphones. Very powerful radio dish receivers are used by governments to communicate with other satellites from facilities known as Earth stations.

As Fast as Light

The signals travel at the same speed. They zoom through space at the speed of light, which is more than 186,000 miles per second (300,000 kps). However, each GPS signal arrives at a receiver on Earth at a slightly different time. This is because some satellites are farther away from the receiver than others.

Calculations on Earth

Back on Earth, to calculate the receiver's position, the GPS receiver (which, for example, could be a handheld device, a smartphone, or a car's GPS system) detects signals from four of the GPS satellites. The receiver then calculates the distance to each of the four satellites by measuring how long it took for the signal to reach it. The time difference between radio signals from four satellites is compared and then, using advanced math, the GPS receiver can calculate its exact position on Earth.

HIGH-TECH HISTORY

In 1988, the Magellan company released the Magellan NAV 1000. It was the first handheld GPS receiver that was available for anyone to buy. It weighed around 1.5 pounds (0.7 kg), was powered by a battery that only lasted a few hours, and it cost around $3,000. In 1999, the Japanese company Casio launched the Casio Pro Trek Satellite Navi. It was the first wristwatch to include GPS and it displayed navigational data on a monochrome LCD screen. It was also far cheaper, costing around one-tenth of the price of a Magellan NAV 1000.

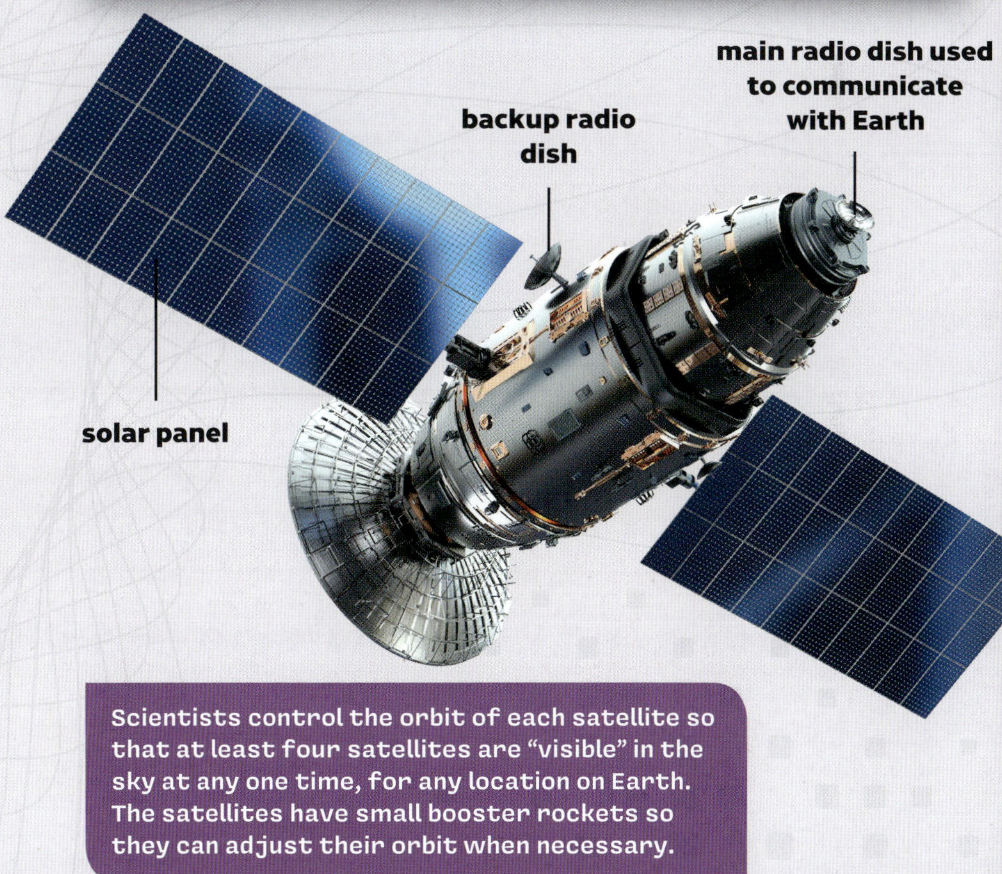

Scientists control the orbit of each satellite so that at least four satellites are "visible" in the sky at any one time, for any location on Earth. The satellites have small booster rockets so they can adjust their orbit when necessary.

A Lesson in Math

A GPS receiver does some very smart math to figure out its position on Earth. This calculation is called trilateration. The easiest way to understand trilateration is to picture it on a flat surface rather than in three-dimensional (3-D) space.

Here's How It Works

Imagine you are lost. You need reference points to find out where you are. The first reference, called point A, is 100 miles (160 km) away from your location. To figure out where you are, you will need a piece of paper, a compass, and a pencil.

Imagine that 1 inch (2.5 cm) on the paper is 10 miles (16 km) on Earth. Using the compass, draw a circle with a radius of 10 inches (25.4 cm) to represent the 100 miles (160 km) around point A. You know you are at some point on the circumference.

The second reference, point B, is 50 miles (80 km) away from your location. Draw another circle around point B with a radius of 5 inches (12.7 cm) to represent the 50 miles (80 km). You must be at one of the two points where the circles meet.

HIGH-TECH STARS WHO CHANGED THE WORLD

ROGER L. EASTON

Scientist Roger L. Easton (1921–2014) was one of the three key people behind the invention of GPS. In 1957, he created a tracking system to follow the orbits of the United States' early space launch attempts. Two years later, he created the Naval Space Surveillance System, which could track all satellites orbiting Earth. During the next two decades, he worked on the concept of using satellites as navigation tools on Earth. Easton had the breakthrough idea of mounting very precise atomic clocks in satellites. The very first GPS signal was transmitted by an experimental satellite, called NTS-2, in 1977.

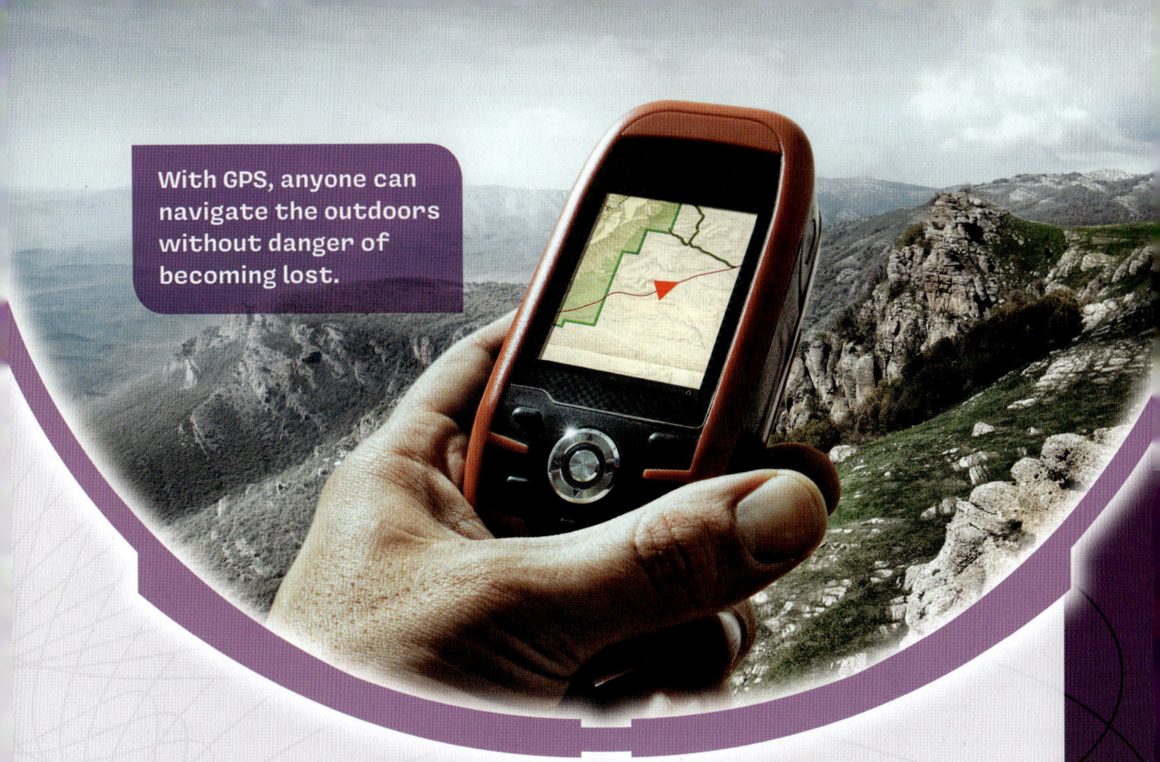

With GPS, anyone can navigate the outdoors without danger of becoming lost.

The Third Circle

The third reference, point C, is 60 miles (100 km) away from your location. Draw a third circle around point C, with a radius of 6 inches (15.2 cm) to represent the 60 miles (100 km). The circumference of this circle will pass through only one of the points where the first two circles meet. You have just found out where you are (see image right)! Trilateration works in the same way in 3-D as it does on a flat surface, but the circles are spheres that overlap.

point C
you
point B
point A

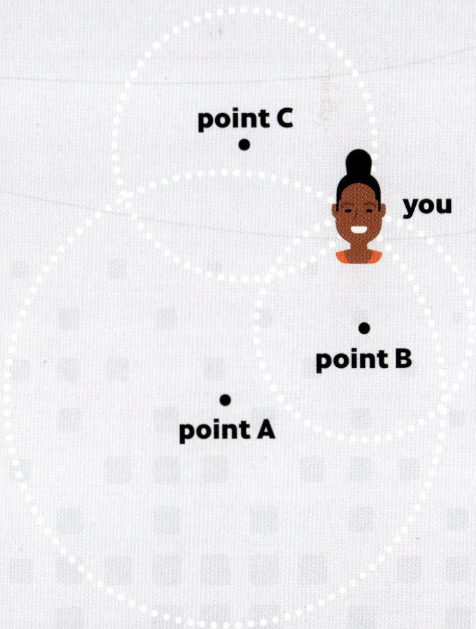

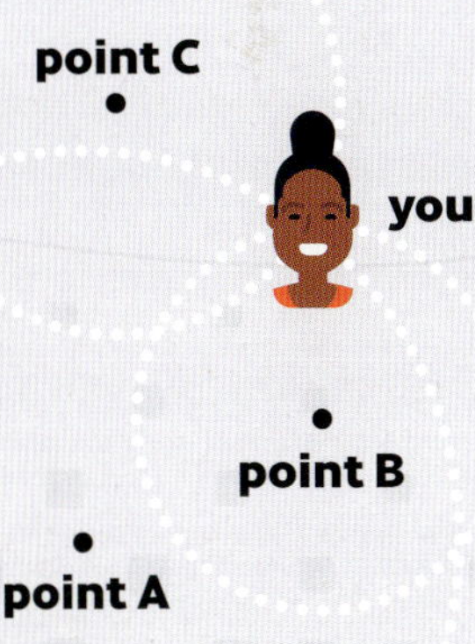

Improved Accuracy

Most GPS receivers receive signals from four or more satellites to calculate the position on Earth. This improves the accuracy of the receiver and can also reveal the receiver's altitude (height above sea level).

CHAPTER 2

A MILITARY START

Many technologies that we take for granted began as military inventions. Satellites, rockets, and GPS were first used only by military forces before the technology changed the lives of ordinary people.

GPS started life in the 1960s as a military technology. It developed as a result of an arms race between the United States and the Soviet Union. Today, the US military uses GPS technology for missile guidance, search and rescue, and enemy surveillance.

Sputnik 1, the first artificial satellite, was a metal ball measuring just 23 inches (58 cm) across. Its four external radio antennae broadcast a very simple, repeating beeping sound.

Spying with Satellites

In 1957, scientists from the Soviet Union sent the world's first satellite, Sputnik 1, into orbit around Earth. This was a huge achievement, but it was also cause for concern. At the time, the United States and the Soviet Union were enemies. The United States believed that the Soviets would use their next satellites to spy on them, and decided to keep an eye on the Soviet satellite. The United States used computers to follow Sputnik 1 as it orbited Earth.

US scientists had already decided to use the same technology to build their own satellites to spy on the Soviets from space.

War and GPS

During the 1960s, the conflict between the Soviet Union and the United States was growing. This period in history is called the Cold War. Both countries built nuclear weapons and threatened to use them against each other. In the following decades, the US government spent billions of dollars on satellite technology. This investment allowed for the development of GPS.

HIGH-TECH HISTORY

In 1983, President Ronald Reagan decided to make GPS available for everyone to use. His decision followed an attack on a South Korean passenger plane shot down by Soviet jets, killing all on board. The South Korean plane may not have strayed into Soviet airspace if the crew had had GPS navigation.

While he was in office (1981–1989), President Reagan was ultimately responsible for GPS. A future president could decide to disable GPS for anyone but the military in the case of war.

GPS in War

GPS technology played a vital role in the success of more recent conflicts such as the Gulf War (1990–1991), the Iraq War (2003–2011), and the Afghanistan War (2001–2021). Today, most modern US military operations rely on GPS technology.

Guidance Without Landmarks

GPS technology was extremely useful during the Gulf, Iraq, and Afghanistan Wars because the regions are so desolate. Soldiers carried handheld GPS receivers to navigate in areas where there were few landmarks to guide them. Using GPS technology, soldiers could also navigate in very poor visibility, for example, at night or during the violent sandstorms common in the Iraq region.

Directing Missiles

Another common use for GPS technology is weapons guidance. A simple GPS receiver converts a conventional gravity bomb into a precision-guided "smart bomb." Military engineers can preprogram smart bombs with the target coordinates. After launch, satellite signals constantly update the missile with its location so it can home in on its target. Because smart bombs rely on computer guidance, they can be used in all conditions, for example, in poor visibility and at night.

The Problem of Jamming

Satellite-guided missiles do not always successfully hit their targets. One of the main reasons for failure is GPS jamming. This is when a GPS jammer disrupts the signals the missiles need to stay on-target. GPS jammers are cheap and easy to use. To overcome this problem, many weapons have a backup, such as heat-seeking infrared systems.

In desert combat zones, GPS is an invaluable navigation tool.

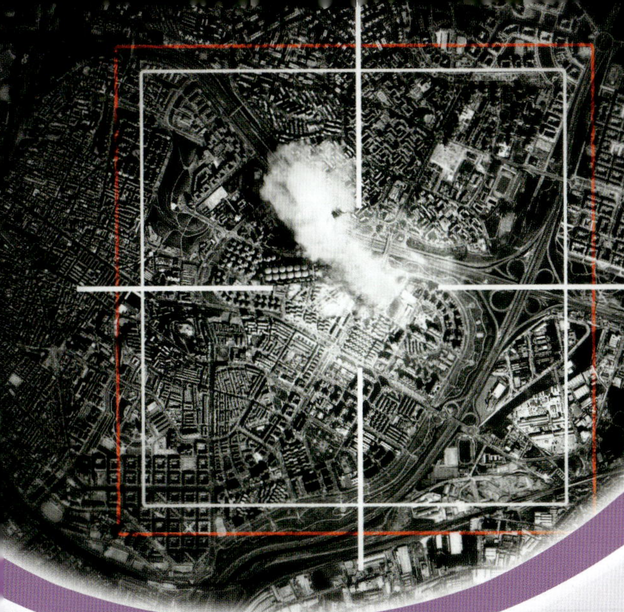

Modern missiles are designed to achieve pinpoint accuracy to avoid civilian casualties. Here, a camera on an orbiting satellite captures the moment a guided missile strikes its target within a city.

HOW HIGH-TECH CHANGED THE WORLD

GPS not only provides an accurate position, the technology can also help distinguish friendly soldiers from enemy troops. Military GPS receivers send out signals to identify soldiers in combat zones. This reduces incidents of friendly fire—when troops accidentally fire on their allies. GPS has helped the military avoid many friendly fire situations, which would have resulted in US soldiers being injured or killed.

GPS can tell soldiers exactly where they are, but can also allow senior officers in a command center to monitor a battle in real time. This can be useful when soldiers need support or rapid medical evacuation by helicopter.

While operating behind enemy lines, soldiers are in unfamiliar territory. They need to know their own precise location in order to accurately identify enemy locations for targeting. This can be achieved far more quickly with GPS than it can with a map and compass.

Spies in the Sky

One of the main military uses of GPS is for surveillance. The GPS satellites orbit thousands of miles above Earth's surface, so they can be used to spy on people without them ever being aware of it. GPS is useful because it can pinpoint your location almost anywhere on the planet. The same technology can also tell you the location of others. Military commanders use GPS surveillance to chart the movements of enemy troops as well as monitor the position of their own forces.

Troop Tracker

US military commanders first used GPS satellite surveillance during the Gulf War. Using GPS, they could track their own soldiers and their vehicles in real time, making it much easier to deploy their forces in the right places. In 1994, the US military developed a portable GPS-based tracking system called the Truth Data Acquisition, Recording, and Display System (TDARDS). This revolutionary system uses a computer, GPS data, and a radio link to provide military commanders with accurate data on the position of aircraft, troops, and ground vehicles.

Behind Enemy Lines

Military GPS surveillance relies on troops working behind enemy lines. The soldiers use GPS systems to fix enemy positions on the ground. The troops then report the position coordinates back to base so that military commanders can use the data to prepare ground or air assaults. The coordinates can also be used to program precision-guided weapons.

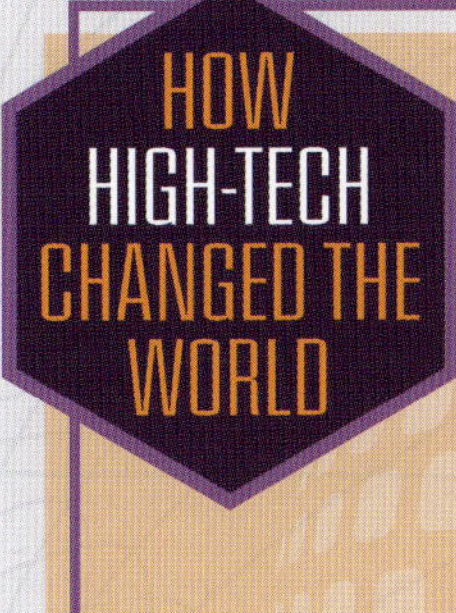

The US military and its allies use a GPS system called Blue Force Tracking (BFT) to provide the location of friendly and hostile military forces. The system also records conditions on the battlefield, such as the location of mines. Soldiers plot data on a computerized map, and the system shares this with other troops in the area. This technology has revolutionized the way the military carries out operations and has saved many lives.

Back at the command center, technical support personnel constantly monitor the precise positions of all soldiers involved in a mission. GPS helps the technical experts see where all squads of troops are located, allowing senior commanders to direct a battle.

Many fighter jets have just one seat, so the pilot also acts as gunner and navigator. US fighters are equipped with GPS, so the pilot can concentrate on flying the aircraft. All civilian jets are also fitted with GPS.

Life and Death

For soldiers in the combat zone, carrying a GPS receiver can mean the difference between life and death. Using GPS, it is much easier to pinpoint the location of lost or wounded soldiers. Rescue teams use the GPS coordinates to speed up the search, which dramatically increases the chances of survival.

On the Grid

Military GPS units map Earth's surface as a grid of squares, each measuring 6 miles (10 km) by 6 miles (10 km). This grid is called the Military Grid Reference System (MGRS). Each square on the grid is given a letter and number. For example, the square covering Chicago is called "16TDM." The precise location of an object within each square is written as a ten-digit coordinate. The coordinates are accurate to within 3 feet (1 m).

Safe Flying

All US military vehicles have inbuilt GPS receivers to reveal their position all the time. This is particularly important for aircraft operating in combat zones, because there is always the chance that they will be shot down by enemy fire. GPS tracking helps reduce the time it takes to find downed aircraft because the GPS data records the aircraft's last known location, speed, altitude, and direction.

A soldier injured in combat needs medical help as quickly as possible. Sending GPS coordinates to the command center allows for a fast evacuation.

Monitoring Soldier Health

The military also uses GPS to monitor and track the health of soldiers while on missions. The system checks the heartbeat and body temperature of the soldiers, as well as their geographical position.

HOW HIGH-TECH CHANGED THE WORLD

In 2005, the US government approved the use of a GPS-enabled device called the Combat Survivor Evader Locator (CSEL) for military troops. Soldiers in distress can activate the CSEL to transmit their exact location to search-and-rescue services. The soldiers can also exchange information such as the state of their injuries and the position of enemy troops, making rescue missions safer and easier.

Smartphones now have inbuilt GPS. The first GPS-enabled phone was released in 1999. Around the same time, GPS also began appearing in automobiles. Today, GPS is linked to apps such as Google or Apple maps, and many people use them every time they need to find directions.

Not Just the Military

GPS is no longer a technology used only by the military. Today, GPS technology is a common feature of many everyday devices that are used by people around the world. At first, the US military did not want to share the GPS. Military chiefs believed that hostile countries and terrorists would use the new technology against the United States. That is why when the US government made GPS available to everyone, it made the public signals much weaker than the military signals. This inbuilt error was called Selective Availability.

Much More Accurate

With Selective Availability on, the time signal sent by each GPS satellite was not exactly the same. Without knowing this information, the GPS receiver on Earth could not provide a precise location. As a result, Selective Availability made public GPS signals far less accurate than military signals.

In the Modern World

When the Department of Defense (DoD) stopped using Selective Availability on public GPS signals, GPS became more accurate for everyone to use. As a result, GPS receivers became a part of many gadgets, from smartphones to smart watches, giving the public a chance to use a powerful military technology in their everyday lives.

Civilian and Military

Today, the accuracy of GPS signals from space is exactly the same for both civilian and military systems. However, civilian signals broadcast over one radio frequency, while military GPS use two. Using two frequencies increases the accuracy of the military GPS by making the radio signals clearer.

HIGH-TECH STARS WHO CHANGED THE WORLD

BRAD PARKINSON

Brad Parkinson is an inventor and engineer, as well as a retired air force colonel. He was one of the key people who proposed GPS, along with Roger L. Easton and Ivan Getting. It was Parkinson's work that resulted in the military approving the launch of four experimental satellites to test the idea of navigation using space satellites. Decades later, Parkinson was one of the senior scientists operating NASA's Gravity Probe B spacecraft, which performed the first direct test of Albert Einstein's theory of general relativity.

CHAPTER 3

FINDING THE WAY WITH GPS

Ever since the US government gave the public access to GPS, companies have come up with more and more ways to use this technology. One of the main uses is to help people find their way around. GPS navigation is now common in applications ranging from air traffic control and in-car navigation to sports and games such as geocaching.

Navigation for Cars

One of the first GPS success stories is automobile navigation, and GPS navigation is now a standard feature of modern cars. The system is called sat-nav, which is short for satellite-navigation. Sat-nav systems help drivers plan the best route for their journey. They work by using the GPS signals to fix the position of the car on a computerized map, which is stored on a database on the device or accessed via the Internet. The map displays the car's position and the route. The driver can follow the instructions on the screen.

Easy to Use

Sat-nav systems are very easy to use. The driver inputs an address, landmark, or zip code, and the sat-nav system plans the best route to guide them to their destination.

Electronic devices can be a distraction in a car, so car GPS navigation systems are voice operated, hands-free, and relay directions to the driver as voice commands.

The airspace above the United States is the busiest of any country in the world. It will get even busier as demand for air travel increases, and managing this demand would not be possible without GPS.

Most systems have touch screens to make them easier to use when driving, and many include extra information such as nearby gas stations and restaurants. Some even speak to the driver using prerecorded voice commands.

Problems with Sat-Nav

Sat-nav systems have many benefits over traditional maps. However, they also have disadvantages. Drivers can take wrong turns if the maps on the device are out of date. It is important to update the maps to include road closures and other changes. Another disadvantage is that drivers can get lost if they do not check to make sure that their end destination matches the one to which the sat-nav is sending them.

HOW HIGH-TECH CHANGED THE WORLD

The Next Generation Air Transportation System (NextGen) is transforming air traffic control in the United States. NextGen relies on GPS signals to broadcast the precise location of aircraft in the sky and on runways. NextGen allows planes to fly closer together and avoid delays caused by "stacking" as planes wait to land on an open runway.

Construction sites can be dangerous places, so many safety rules are in place for workers. Using GPS, a site coordinator can now see, at a glance, where all the dangerous machines are and can keep people at a safe distance with ease.

GPS in the Workplace

Many different industries use GPS in the workplace. They include construction, in which GPS is used to aid the precise movement of heavy-duty machinery. There are also benefits in the open ocean, where navigation is difficult.

Control in Construction

Heavy-duty construction machinery is often equipped with GPS guidance in order to aid precision movement. It is even possible to use GPS to preprogram the coordinates of foundations and other structures before the construction starts. The accuracy of GPS means construction workers can move a load into the right position on the first attempt.

Accurate Mapping

GPS has transformed construction by helping engineers build accurate site maps. Today, engineers create an electronic map of the construction site and feed in data from the GPS system. In this way, workers on the site can see exactly how far they are digging by comparing the depth of the hole with information on the site map.

HOW HIGH-TECH CHANGED THE WORLD

In the past, sailors relied on maritime charts and complex calculations to navigate on the open ocean. Today, they can use GPS technology to pinpoint their exact position, speed, and direction of travel, to ensure they arrive at their destination. GPS technology also helps sailors navigate through busy ports and waterways.

Finding Fish

GPS technology helps fishing vessels locate the best fishing areas. Programming the coordinates into the GPS device means the vessel can return to the same spot again and again. Some GPS devices combine GPS and sonar technology to recreate maps of the ocean floor. These charts can reveal features such as underwater trenches, which provide ideal hiding places for large shoals of fish.

Ships and boats at sea use a system called Automatic Identification System (AIS), which constantly broadcasts their location, speed, course, and identity. AIS is combined with GPS to give ship captains real-time updates on all the other vessels around them.

Launched in 2009, Strava (see below) has free and subscription versions. By 2020, it had more than 50 million users, who had collectively uploaded 3 billion records of their activities.

GPS Gets Sporty

GPS technology can also be used as a training aid to increase performance in many different sports, from cycling and mountain biking to marathon running. GPS receivers are cheap, light, and small, and they have also been built into devices as small as smartphones and wristwatches. GPS technology has become a useful training tool for athletes. GPS devices can record the distance covered, time spent exercising, and average speed reached during training. The data can then be downloaded onto a computer to assess an athlete's performance and fitness.

GPS for Training

Some companies have developed apps that use GPS technology to record training sessions. Strava is an app that has become popular with cyclists and runners. The app uses GPS technology to record how quickly an athlete can ride or run a section of a course. The athlete uploads the data onto the Strava website and can see how they have performed against other athletes.

A Neat Fit

The first GPS receivers were large and heavy to carry around, which was not ideal for mountaineers or hikers on a long trip. Today, GPS receivers have been built into devices as small as wristwatches. Innovations such as surface mount technology (SMT) and robotic assembly have shrunk GPS receivers onto tiny circuit boards so they can fit into smaller and smaller spaces.

HOW HIGH-TECH CHANGED THE WORLD

Along with using GPS, modern smartphones have help with pinpointing their location. Assisted Global Positioning System (AGPS) is a system through which your phone pings the nearest cell phone communication towers to find your location. It is not as accurate as satellite GPS but, when combined, GPS with AGPS can update your location faster. The cell phone towers are much closer to your phone than the GPS satellites, so your phone receives a stronger radio signal from them. The location accuracy from the towers depends on how strong the signal is. However, unlike GPS, AGPS does use some data on your phone.

Using GPS on a bicycle ride helps people check their exercise progress.

Geocaching and geodashing both rely on GPS devices. In geodashing, the locations or dashpoints are used for one game only until the game is over. Geocaching uses locations that are permanent.

Games and GPS

Some people have developed games that make use of GPS technology. One game is called geocaching. This treasure-hunting game uses GPS to locate containers, called geocaches, which are hidden by other players in the game.

Find the Treasure

People playing geocaching use GPS-enabled devices such as smartphones and GPS receivers. They use GPS to navigate to a set of coordinates and then find the hidden geocache at that location. Most geocaches are just a waterproof box containing a logbook. Players then sign the book to show they have found the "treasure." Some people hide more valuable items, such as books and toys. One of the rules of geocaching says that if you take an item from the geocache, you must replace it with something of equal or greater value. This means that the next person to find the geocache is not disappointed with the treasure.

All Over the World

People have hidden geocaches all over the world. The treasure could be up a tree in your local park, on the side of the street, or even underwater. Once the geocache is in position, the player posts it on a website like www.geocaching.com. People use the site to find out about hidden geocaches in their area and head off to find them. When the player finds one, they can record the find in the logbook or on the cache page on the site.

GPS Gaming

Geodashing is another popular GPS game. It involves teams of players using GPS receivers to find random "dashpoints" as quickly as they can. The first person to reach the dashpoint wins the game for their team. Geodashing started in 2001, and the first game lasted two months, from the start of June to the end of July. Since then most games have lasted just one month from start to finish.

DR GLADYS WEST

Earth, like the other planets, is not a perfect sphere. Dr Gladys West is a mathematician best known for her work on measuring the exact shape of Earth using measurements from satellites. In her early career she worked for the Naval Proving Ground, and was only the second Black woman ever employed by them. Before measuring Earth's shape, she had worked on proving that Neptune orbited the sun three times for every two orbits that Pluto made. In 2018, she was inducted into the US Air Force Hall of Fame. Her work on the shape of Earth was vital to early GPS satellites.

CHAPTER 4

GPS MAPS THE WORLD

Before GPS, mapmaking was a time-consuming process that involved weeks or even months of painstaking measuring and recording. Then all that information had to be drawn and labeled to create a paper map. GPS technology has made mapmaking much easier. People can now draw maps on the spot using GPS receivers, computers, and traditional surveying tools.

Modern Maps

GPS technology provides the precise coordinates to plot modern maps with amazing accuracy. Because the data from GPS satellites is instant, surveyors can plot coordinates immediately. Surveyors carry their GPS systems in backpacks or vehicles so they can collect the data as quickly as possible. They can then combine this data with the information from surveying techniques, such as trilateration (see pages 10–11).

A geographical information system (GIS) is a type of map that displays data as a series of layers (see opposite).

Layers and Layers

GIS maps are electronic files, and they display everything from highway routes to local services such as gas stations and convenience stores. Unlike traditional maps, a GIS displays all the geographical data about an area. Each layer represents one type of data, such as all the highways or all the service stations in a particular area. You can turn layers on or off to narrow down what you want to see. GIS technology is constantly improving, so a GIS conference is held every year at which people can meet to share information.

Keeping up to Date

One of the biggest advantages of GPS mapping over paper maps is that GPS maps can be updated regularly. This is important because the network of roads and highways is constantly changing. It is easy to update a digital file on a GPS mapping system as new bypasses are built and more lanes are added to existing roads and highways.

HOW HIGH-TECH CHANGED THE WORLD

People can now create their own maps. They do so using GPS receivers and web utilities such as www.gpsvisualizer.com. These sites collect the data from GPS-enabled devices to create maps of where people have been, plan where they want to go, and some even suggest where to stop off for lunch.

GPS Visualizer began more than 20 years ago and is currently used by people worldwide to create several thousand new customized maps every day. One user-created example is a map that plots plant species seen on forest walks.

A Scientist's Best Friend

Scientists are using GPS technology to help them with their research. Some use the technology to measure the impact of human activities on wildlife and the environment. Others use satellite data to study and map areas of particular historical interest.

Saving the World

Environmental scientists study the impact of human activities on the environment. They monitor the effects of industries, such as farming and mining, on certain habitats. They feed in coordinates from GPS data onto satellite maps to record the damage these activities are having on the environment. By using GPS data, environmental scientists have mapped deforestation in the Amazon rain forest and the melting of the polar ice caps.

HIGH-TECH STARS WHO CHANGED THE WORLD

IVAN GETTING

Ivan Getting (1912–2003) was a scientist and engineer. During World War II (1939–1945), he developed a fire-control radar that allowed missiles aimed at London, United Kingdom (UK), to be shot down with much more success than was possible before. He later worked on a guidance system to allow nuclear missiles to be launched from a mobile railcar without losing accuracy. His work in tracking objects moving quickly in 3-D space was a critical step toward GPS. Along with his colleagues Roger L. Easton and Brad Parkinson, Ivan Getting was one of the main creators of GPS.

A GPS wildlife-tracking collar is specially designed so it does not disrupt an animal's normal activities.

Saving Animals

Conservationists study and protect endangered wildlife. One way to do this is to attach GPS receivers to wildlife in the form of collars or tags. These devices are then used to track the animals in the wild in real time. This helps the conservationists plan ways to protect wildlife from danger. Similarly, some people use the same GPS technology to track their pets, so they do not get lost.

Fighting Wildfires

GPS technology is also used to help protect the planet. In Australia, wildfires are a constant threat in the scorching summer. Firefighters fly over a fire in helicopters mounted with GPS receivers to map the extent of the fires. Then they can plan how to put them out. GPS has revolutionized firefighting, helping to more quickly tackle blazes and therefore save property and lives.

As well as mapping harmful wildfires, GPS is also used to track firefighting vehicles so they can quickly be deployed to the areas where they are needed.

CHAPTER 5

RESCUING AND TRACKING

Most emergency services rely on GPS technology for search-and-rescue operations. By carrying a GPS receiver, teams involved in rescue operations can identify the location of the person in distress and plan a speedy response.

A Lifesaver

In 2011, a devastating earthquake hit Japan. GPS technology saved many lives in the aftermath. Emergency search-and-rescue teams used GPS combined with satellite images to map the disaster areas and plan their rescue efforts. The earthquake destroyed visible landmarks, such as bridges and highways, so GPS was an ideal way to coordinate the search-and-rescue effort.

GPS works no matter where you are—as long as three GPS satellites are above your horizon, your exact location can be pinpointed. If four are above your horizon, your altitude can be determined too.

Into Europe

Countries from the European Union (EU) now have their own satellite navigation system. Called Galileo, it also provides a search-and-rescue function. The Galileo satellites are fitted with a transponder, which is a device that transmits and receives radio signals. The transponder transfers distress signals to rescue coordination centers, which then initiate the search-and-rescue mission. At the same time, the transponder sends a response signal to the person in distress to let them know help is on the way.

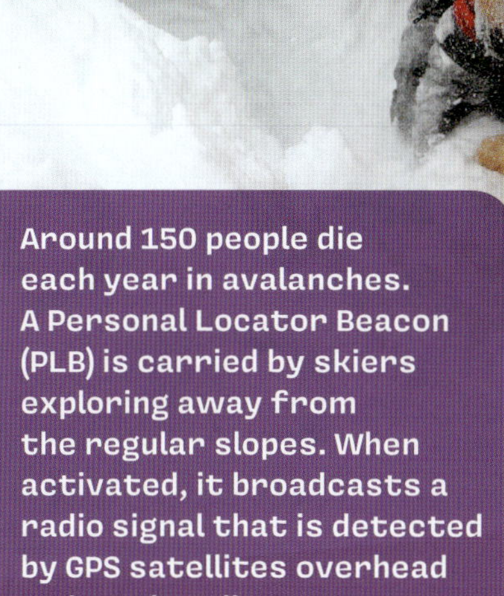

Around 150 people die each year in avalanches. A Personal Locator Beacon (PLB) is carried by skiers exploring away from the regular slopes. When activated, it broadcasts a radio signal that is detected by GPS satellites overhead and used to direct rescuers.

Aided by GPS

Most smartphones now contain GPS receivers. People who enjoy activities such as hiking and mountaineering use mobile apps like Outdooractive to find their way around, but also to broadcast where they are at all times. If they find themselves in trouble, the GPS signal can lead an emergency team directly to their location. The system even works in remote places with no cell phone signals.

HOW HIGH-TECH CHANGED THE WORLD

Scientists from the National Aeronautics and Space Administration (NASA) estimate that it takes fewer than 5 minutes to detect and locate distress signals using the Distress Alerting Satellite System (DASS). This system relays the signals to emergency teams using GPS satellites.

Preventing Tragedy

Scientists use GPS technology to predict earthquakes and tsunamis to prevent the huge loss of life that often accompany these natural disasters. Japan lies on the Pacific Ring of Fire, an area that experiences a lot of volcanic and earthquake activity. As a result, the country has been hit by some of the most devastating earthquakes in history. Japanese scientists are using a network of GPS sensors called GEONET to measure the underground movements that cause these violent earthquakes. The GPS data can be used to predict the size and strength of the quake, and also where it will strike.

Big Wave Hunter

Scientists study GPS data from ships and ocean buoy sensors to measure underwater earthquakes that trigger tsunamis. The sensors detect the forces that shake the ocean floor and set the tsunami in motion. The data is then used to measure the location of the quake and predict the areas where a tsunami will strike.

Tsunamis can cause devastation. When underwater tremors hit the floating sensors off the coast of Japan, they make them move up and down. The movement is measured and authorities are alerted instantly, allowing more time for evacuations.

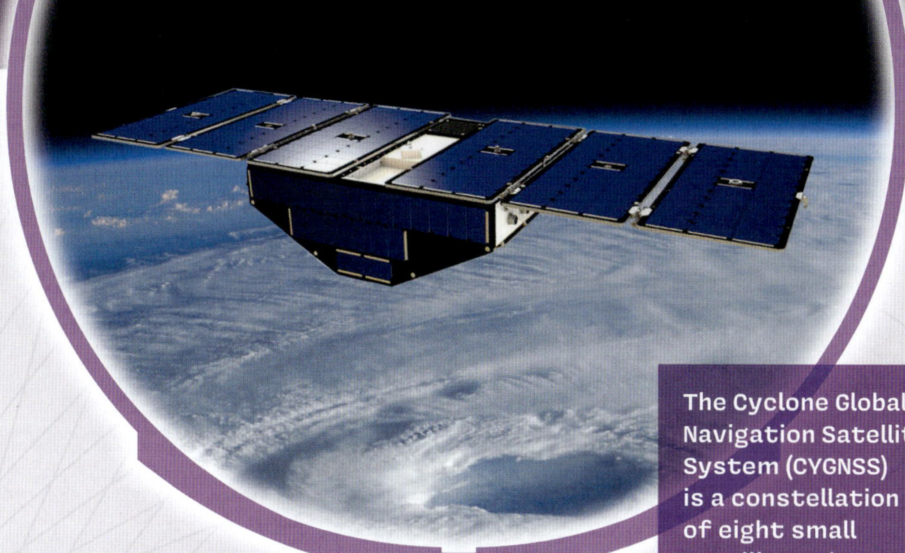

The Cyclone Global Navigation Satellite System (CYGNSS) is a constellation of eight small satellites that use GPS to monitor tropical storms. This smart system examines GPS radio signals that have reflected from Earth's oceans. These reflected signals change depending on how rough the water is.

Watching the Weather

People who study the weather are called meteorologists. These scientists also use GPS sensors to predict the weather so that news stations and weather websites can provide the public with a weather forecast. They study the radio signals from GPS satellites as they travel through Earth's atmosphere. For example, the GPS signals slow down in moist air, which may suggest that a storm is building.

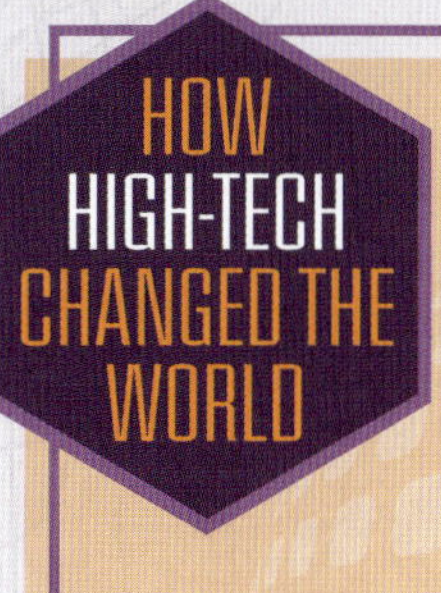

Predicting weather and natural disasters has been made far more efficient thanks to GPS. Today, meteorologists use the GPS data from special devices called dropsondes to predict hurricanes. They release the dropsonde into the eye of the hurricane and the GPS receiver broadcasts the speed and direction of the storm. This can help predict where and when the hurricane is likely to hit.

CHAPTER 6

TRACKED BY GPS

GPS technology is not just used for navigation, it can also be used to track objects and people, from delivery vehicles and buses and trains on public transit systems to criminals on their smartphones.

Data Pushers

Many freight companies use GPS receivers as tracking devices on delivery vehicles. Some units are data loggers, which simply record the movements of vehicles and store the data as an electronic file. Other devices are data pushers, which use a cell phone to send, or "push," the data back to a computer at the warehouse.

Easy Tracking

Companies use GPS trackers to check on the progress of deliveries so they can advise customers when they will receive their goods. This is called fleet tracking. The information from the GPS units serves another purpose too—it can be used to check on employees to ensure they are doing their jobs well.

Truck drivers use GPS for navigation and the owner of the cargo container uses it to track their property. The container has its own GPS, so it can be tracked when it is transferred to train or cargo ship.

Smartphones are expensive to replace when lost or stolen. As long as a phone is turned on, it is receiving GPS signals. People can log in to their account on another device and see their lost phone on a map.

HOW HIGH-TECH CHANGED THE WORLD

Apple's iPhone has an app called Find My iPhone that uses GPS signals to locate lost or stolen phones. In 2023, police in California arrested five people who had committed an armed robbery on a jewelry store. They stole jewelry worth more than $1 million, including a Rolex watch that had a GPS tracker hidden in its packaging. That led police directly to the watch and thieves.

Keeping on Time

Public transit networks use a similar system to fleet tracking to ensure bus and train services run on time. Computers track GPS signals from receivers on buses and trains on the network, and compare the location of each vehicle to the published schedule. If a bus or train is running late, the display can be shown to passengers waiting at the next stop. That helps passengers monitor when the bus or train will arrive.

Catching Criminals

Today's law-enforcement officers are turning to GPS to help them catch criminals. They are using the information from GPS devices to provide evidence that could convict a suspect in the courtroom. For example, detectives use GPS tracking devices and the data from automobile sat-nav systems to follow suspects who are on the move. This can help detectives build up evidence about a person that may be useful in securing a conviction—for example, by placing a suspect at the scene of a crime.

Convicting Criminals

During their investigation of a 2019 murder case, police discovered photos of one of the suspects running a marathon a few years earlier—while wearing a GPS smart watch. They found the smart watch during a search of his house, and took it for analysis. The watch data showed that the suspect had traveled close to the victim's home months before the planned murder, to plot an escape route. This helped convict the killer.

A criminal can be caught on CCTV, but may still be impossible to identify. If they have a smartphone or smart watch, the devices will have recorded their exact movements and location and can be used to prove their guilt.

HIGH-TECH HISTORY

One of the first criminal convictions with the help of GPS took place in 2008, when police in Chicago used the GPS data from an automobile sat-nav system to help convict a murderer named Eric Hanson. The police downloaded the GPS data from his sat-nav system to place him at the scene of the brutal murder of his family in 2005. Hanson was sentenced to death for his crime.

A criminal can turn their phone off before committing a crime while on foot. But a criminal using a car will have recorded their activity in the car's GPS device. This recorded data can be used to help convict them.

Jammed Up

Criminals are now wising up to the threat of GPS. They are using devices called GPS jammers to block the signals from tracking devices to avoid detection. GPS jammers are cheap and easy to buy (some cost less than $100), and some websites even show people how to build their own device. These jamming devices are effective because the signals received from GPS satellites are very weak.

Tracking Danger

Some countries are using GPS technology to help monitor the movements of convicted criminals who might pose a danger to the public. They must wear GPS tags so the authorities can keep track of their movements. Criminals who commit minor crimes can escape a jail sentence if they agree to wear an electronic tag. These tags broadcast the exact location of the people wearing them to the authorities. Using tags, police can follow criminals 24 hours a day to ensure they do not commit more crimes.

Tagged for Tracking

A GPS tag is simply a strong plastic strap that contains a GPS receiver. The tag is usually worn around the ankle and is almost impossible to remove. The GPS tag also contains a special circuit that, if broken by a particularly determined criminal, sends a signal to inform the police.

Tag Rules

Sometimes, a judge in court may impose certain restrictions on a prisoner who has served a prison sentence and is being released back into society. These restrictions may put limits on the time the offender is allowed to be out of their home—for example, a person wearing a tag may not be allowed out after 6pm and before 7am every day.

Electronic Monitoring (EM) ankle tags are similar to wildlife tracking collars —they are comfortable, waterproof, and robust in design. Unlike wildlife tracking collars, they have batteries that require regular charging. Allowing the battery to run out is a breach of the conditions imposed on the wearer.

Stopping Offending

GPS tags can reveal all the information that a regular GPS receiver can show, such as the offender's precise location and the direction and speed they are going. The tags can also be used to enforce "exclusion zones" to prevent offenders going somewhere they are not allowed to be under the rules of the court. That has helped monitor and control offender behavior, preventing potential criminal acts.

HIGH-TECH STARS WHO CHANGED THE WORLD

ALBERT EINSTEIN

Albert Einstein (1879–1955) was a German scientist best known for his theories of relativity. His work led to the concept of time dilation. We may think that time ticks at the same rate everywhere and for everything, but Einstein showed that, for objects moving very fast, time appears to slow down for anyone observing it. For GPS satellites orbiting Earth at thousands of miles per hour, this can have a tiny-but-measurable effect. Therefore, Einstein's work must be taken into account by GPS, otherwise its measurement of a location would very quickly become inaccurate by as much as 6 miles (10 km) in just one day!

CONCLUSION

A HIGH-TECH FUTURE

Until a few decades ago, the GPS was available only for military use. Hardly anyone knew about the network of GPS satellites circling high above Earth's surface. Today, it is difficult to imagine a world without GPS. This incredible technology is likely to become even more powerful and transformative in the future.

Better GPS

The US government is spending billions of dollars upgrading the GPS. It is launching a new generation of GPS satellites to boost the signals and make the system more accurate. The United States is also working closely with European countries to ensure GPS works with their new Galileo navigation system.

Sputnik 1, the first artificial satellite, simply transmitted radio beeps to prove to the world that it was in orbit. Today's satellites power global communication, television, and the Internet, as well as GPS navigation. Satellites have made the world more accessible to everyone.

Self-driving cars are equipped with cameras and other sensors, including lasers and ultrasound. This equipment constantly measures the car's immediate surroundings, other cars, and any hazards. However, to find their location on a map, self-driving cars use GPS.

Apps for Better Living

Most modern smartphones come with GPS receivers as standard. This has led to a huge range of GPS apps that are designed to improve our lives. Some apps use GPS data to suggest local services such as stores and restaurants based on where you are. Social media sites such as Facebook and X are also using GPS data to help locate nearby family and friends of users.

Changing Our Future

As the GPS continues to develop, people will use this amazing technology to change our lives in new ways. Sat-nav systems are already used to guide drivers to their destination. Self-driving cars are still new, but they use GPS to help cars drive without human control. Very soon, all the driver will need to do is key the destination into the device and the car will drive itself there!

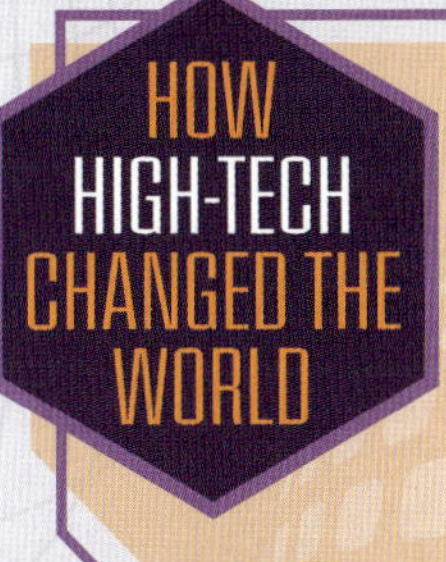

Locata is a different type of positioning technology that is changing the world. It uses ground-based equipment instead of satellites to send a radio signal over a certain area. This signal is about 1 million times stronger than a GPS signal, making Locata much more accurate and reliable.

GLOSSARY

antennae rodlike or disc-shaped devices used to transmit or receive radio waves

app short for application software, a program that tells a computer or other electronic device to do something

artificial made by people and not naturally occurring

atomic clock an extremely accurate device that uses the tiny vibrations of atoms to tell the time

breach to break a rule

circumference the boundary of a circle

civilian a person who is not involved with the military

conservationists scientists who study and protect endangered wildlife

constellations groupings of satellites that work together

convict to be declared guilty of committing a crime

coordinates numbers that represent the position of an object, such as a person, on Earth's surface

customized changed to suit a particular preference or need

deploy to put into action or use

evacuation the organized movement of people away from an area due to oncoming dangers and threats

hostile threatening and not friendly

maritime related to the oceans

navigation the process of finding out your location and following a route to a destination

radio signals messages passed through the air in the form of waves of electromagnetic radiation

radius the distance from the center of a circle to the circumference

remote far away from towns and cities and not easy to get to

satellites spacecraft that orbit Earth or another planet

solar panels structures that contain light-sensitive cells that convert the energy from sunlight into electricity

sonar using sound waves to detect objects

surveillance spying on objects or people without anyone knowing about it

surveyors people who figure out the position of things on Earth's surface

touch screens visual displays you can touch to control electronic equipment such as computers and smartphones

trilateration a mathematical calculation used to figure out a location by measuring the distances to known objects

tropical related to the tropics, which are areas of the planet directly north or south of the equator. The equator is an imaginary line that runs around the center of Earth

tsunamis large waves caused by underwater earthquakes. Tsunamis cause widespread damage when they crash onto the shore

FIND OUT MORE

Books

Billings, Tanner. *Rockets and Satellites in Warfare* (STEM in the Military). Cavendish Square Publishing, 2022.

Lew, Kristi. *Inventing GPS* (Amazing Inventions). Focus Readers, 2021.

Markovics, Joyce. *Satellites* (Tech Bytes: Exploring Space). Norwood House Press, 2023.

Websites

The award-winning How Stuff Works website explains how GPS receivers work. Find it at:
electronics.howstuffworks.com/gadgets/travel/gps.htm

The National Geographic website summarizes GPS and its applications at:
education.nationalgeographic.com/education/encyclopedia/gps/?ar_a=1

Explore the official US government website about the GPS and related topics. Click on the "Students" link for tutorials, videos, a poster, and even more at:
www.gps.gov

Publisher's note to educators and parents:
All the websites featured above have been carefully reviewed to ensure that they are suitable for students. However, many websites change often, and we cannot guarantee that a site's future contents will continue to meet our high standards of educational value. Please be advised that students should be closely monitored whenever they access the Internet.

INDEX

ABOUT THE AUTHOR

Kelly Roberts has written many children's science and technology books. She uses GPS on almost every car journey she makes, and the amazing technology has certainly changed her world—and stopped her from getting lost!